I am LOVED

Soy AMADO

Carlota Arriola Rodela

Gabriel S. Gaytan, Illustrator

© 2021 Carlota Arriola Rodela

ISBN 978-1-7352317-7-8

For ages: 5+

Publisher: Ruta Sevo, momox.org

Title font: Adam Scribble from Medialoot (licensed)
Text font: Leander (licensed)
Cover illustration: Gabriel S. Gaytán, gaytanartworks.com

All rights reserved. No part of this book may be used or reproduced without permission.

When we lived in the city junk yard my mom loved me so much that she collected and sold things from there to buy food to feed me.

Cuando vivíamos en el basurero municipal me sentía muy amada porque mi mamá vendía artículos reciclables para vender y darnos de comer.

I am so loved that when people saw how poor we were, they came to help us. The Adrian Dominican Sisters found a center for us where we could be safe.

Me siento muy felíz cuando las monjas nos ayudan cuando ven nuestras necesidades ofreciéndonos trabajo.

We are so loved that the sisters fed us and kept us safe. They helped me to go to school, and they helped my mom learn to sew to make handicrafts to sell to make money for us.

Me siento muy amado por las monjas porque me mandaron a la escuela y ayudaron a mi mamá a que aprendiera a coser.

My mom also got help to go to school. She got to choose to be a teacher assistant or a nurse assistant.

Le ofrecieron a mi mamá oportunidades para escoger una carrera de asistente de maestras o asistente de enfermera.

I am so loved that at the Centro Santa Catalina teachers help me with my school homework after I get back from school.

Me siento tan amado siempre porque las monjas me ayudan con mis tareas y siempre están pendientes de mí.

I am so loved that I can play with my friends in a playground where I feel safe.

Me siento en un ambiente cariñoso cuando juego con mis amigos en el patio de recreo.

I feel so loved that I try my best to help my brothers and sisters when they ask me for help.

Cuando ayudo a mis hermanos y compañeros me siento seguro y amado.

I feel so loved that I try my best when I do my chores and my school work.

Cuando hago mis tareas y mis quehaceres de la casa me siento maravillosa.

I feel loved at the Centro Santa Catalina when I receive gifts at Christmas time and when we go Christmas caroling.

Cuando cantamos en el Centro Santa Catalina las posadas nos sentimos muy amados.

I feel so loved when I see that my mom, my family and my friends are safe and happy.

Cuando mi familia y mis amigos estamos juntos me siento segura y felíz.

About This Story

This is a story about children who lived in abject poverty with their mothers in a waste dump site in Ciudad Juárez, México. The children realized they were loved because they saw how their mothers gathered objects from around the waste dump to sell so they could survive. The children told about how several sisters and lay people came together to actually help them to move into a center where the children and their mothers got help. The children got to go to school and to have a safe place to play before and after school, they told about how their mother got to learn how to sew to make items to sell so she could support herself and her family. The children felt loved by all of the actions taken to help them and their mothers to have a better life.

Centro Santa Catalina

I dedicate this book to the generous lay people and Adrian Dominican Sisters who started a non-profit organization (Centro Santa Catalina) to help women and children remain together in their family units, to gain work skills, to attend school and to become self-sufficient. I also dedicate this book to the parents who work diligently to produce handcrafted items for sale to sustain themselves and their family. This dedication also is for the mother's and children's commitment to their school studies to better themselves. The work the lay people and the nuns do to help the beneficiaries of this center inspired me to write this book. My inspiration is to let the mothers and children know that they are loved by many people in many ways.

https://www.centrosantacatalina.org/

About the Author

Carlota Arriola Rodela was born in El Paso, Texas after her parents immigrated from México. She grew up speaking Spanish and English. All her early schooling, through university, was in El Paso, Texas. Later she got an M.A. at the University of Louisville and a reading certificate at George Mason University.

Her whole career was practicing speech pathology in elementary schools. She enjoys working with children and using literature to connect with children of all ages.

She is married to Eduardo S. Rodela and they live in Fairfax, Virginia. They have a son, Eddie, who lives in Baltimore with his spouse Marisa, and a daughter, Marisela, who lives with her spouse Jeff in Washington DC.

About the Artist/Illustrator

Gabriel S. Gaytán, a native of El Paso, Texas and a UTEP graduate has dedicated himself as a visual artist and educator. Gabriel explores his cultural heritage through images and symbols. Gabriel's Mesoamerican ancestors used colors and symbols to create their artistic language and a revival of this ancient literacy is a dominant theme in his work. Gabriel's work graces the walls of many private collections and public buildings in Texas, New Mexico, Nevada and California. His murals are on display on several I-10 freeway pillars at Lincoln Park in El Paso, Texas.

http://gaytanartworks.com/

gabriel@gaytanartworks.com

Acknowledgements

The author wishes to express her grateful thanks to Ruta Sevo, literary writer and friend. Ruta your project management, and writing skills were of great help in getting this book together, thank you. I want to thank my sister Angélica A. Gaytán for helping me with the Spanish translation. I extend my gratitude also to Gabriel S. Gaytán who so graciously accepted my challenge to illustrate this book with heartfelt enthusiasm. Finally, I acknowledge and thank my spouse Eduardo S. Rodela for encouraging me and helping me through any technological challenges.

Made in the USA
Las Vegas, NV
26 February 2021